Contents

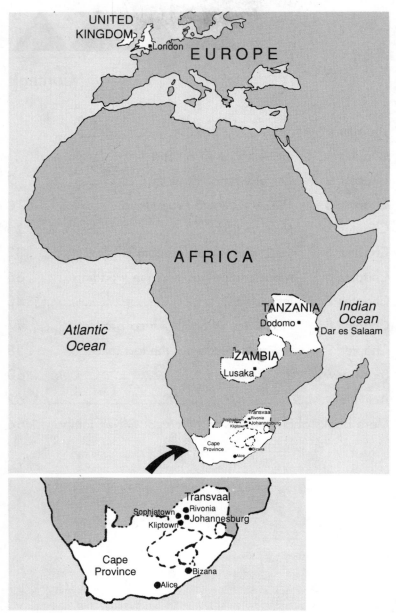

Important places in Oliver Tambo's life

They Fought

Maskew Miller Longman (Pty) Ltd,
Howard Drive, Pinelands, Cape Town

Offices in Johannesburg, Durban, Port Elizabeth, Kimberley,
King William's Town, Pietersburg, Nelspruit and Mafikeng, and
representatives throughout southern Africa.

First published 1994
Second impression 1996

ISBN 0 636 01984 5

Book and cover design by Nina Jawitz
Map by Anne Westoby
Set in 11 on 13pt Sabon
Typesetting and layout by Beverley Visser
Imagesetting and scanning by Castle Graphics
Printed by CTP Book Printers (Pty) Ltd,
Caxton Street, Parow 7500, Cape Town

R5841/RM4769

Acknowledgements

The authors and publishers would like to thank the following organisations and
individuals for the use of photographs and archival material:

The Mayibuye Centre and the Archives, Institute for Historical Research, University
of the Western Cape and Luli Callinicos.

Every effort has been made to trace the owners of copyright material, but in some
cases this has not been possible. The publisher would be glad to hear from any further copyright owners so that appropriate arrangements can be made.

Other books in this series:

Steve Biko	Yusuf Dadoo	Seretse Khama
Z K Matthews	Sol Plaatje	Mohandas Gandhi
Chris Hani		

Titles in preparation:

Abdul Abdurahman	Dora Tamana	Helen Joseph	Braam Fischer
Edwin Mofutsanyana	Albert Luthuli	David Webster	John Dube
Matthew Goniwe	James Calata	Lillian Ngoyi	Ruth First
Dorothy Zihlangu	Cissie Gool	James la Guma	

The return

In February 1990 Oliver Tambo heard the news that he had been waiting for almost all his life. The South African Government had unbanned the African National Congress (ANC). Political prisoners would be released. Thousands of exiles living all over the world would soon be allowed to return home to the land of their birth. The South African Government would begin talks with the ANC and other political groups to plan for the country's first ever democratic elections.

For Oliver Tambo the end of a bitter struggle had finally begun. He was over seventy and almost as old as the ANC itself. He had served the Congress under Dr Xuma, Dr Moroka and Albert Luthuli and as the leader of the ANC.

Of course there were many phone calls of congratulations from all over the world: from his wife Adelaide and children, comrades, friends, presidents and prime ministers.

But while telephones were ringing and letters, telegrams and faxes were pouring in, he must have found a quiet moment to gather his thoughts and to think back to when and where it had all started for him. Oliver Tambo was such a man: he thought hard and carefully before making a decision. And afterwards he examined carefully the results of his actions. He must surely have cast his mind back to the time when he was appointed to lead the ANC during its long years in exile.

Oliver Tambo agreed with the wise person who said that the biggest journeys we take begin with the smallest steps. And so he must have thought back even further to the year 1917 and to a small place in the Eastern Cape called Bizana . . .

A rural village, very similar to Kantolo, where Oliver Tambo spent his childhood

Oliver Tambo's paternal grandparents were born and raised in the Harding district of Natal, on the banks of the Umtanvuna River which borders on the Cape Province.

At some time in their lives this couple moved their home across the river into the Cape Province. It is not known why they made this decision, but we can safely assume that it was for a better life.

Oliver's father, Mzimeni Manchi, was already a young man when this move took place. He found employment at a trading store known as the Ntlazukazi Store. The white owner of the store had named it after a river that flows past the store and meets the Umtanvuna River.

Mzimeni spent many hours selling bags of mealies and other products to the surrounding farms and villages. But in moments when there was nothing to do he would cast his eyes across the Ntlazukazi to the other side. And on a day when the sun was not piercingly hot and obscuring his vision, he could see for miles around. Whenever he looked across the Ntlazukazi his eyes would gradually lift upwards as they slowly followed the slope of a hill. Half way up the hill he would rest his gaze. Here the hill suddenly broke into a saddle, like the landing on a flight of stairs. There, Mzimeni decided, is where I shall build my house and raise a family.

Mzimeni fulfilled his dream and it was here, in a little place called Kantolo (for it can hardly be called a village) where Oliver Tambo was born on 27 October 1917.

The closest town to Kantolo was Bizana. A few years later little Oliver would first set his curious eyes on Bizana and wonder at the dust raised by the wooden wheels of oxcarts and the clip-clop of horses.

Oliver Tambo's father had three wives. To have more than one wife was encouraged as this helped increase the wealth of the homestead*.

But to have even one wife was no simple matter. The groom had to pay lobola* to his future in-laws – a bride price which had to be made in cattle. This forced many men to leave their kraals to work on the Natal sugar plantations or in the bowels of the earth far away on the gold mines of Johannesburg.

Having two or three wives sometimes led to jealousies and petty fights among these wives and their many children. But this was not so in young Oliver's homestead. His mother and stepmothers all got on very well together. This meant that little Oliver – who was named Kaizana at birth – could play and eat at any mother's hut and so he grew up in a homestead that bustled and sang with the work songs of women, the laughter of brothers and sisters and the noise of work and play from dawn to dusk.

The homestead was a cluster of several huts that made up a kraal. Scattered around their kraal were kraals belonging to other families. Some of these kraals were as big as the Tambo kraal, but most were smaller, consisting only of two or three huts. This depended on the size of the families.

Life began very early for the boys and girls in Kantolo: early in the morning, but early in another sense too. At the age of four they were taken away from the comfort of the home and their mother's soothing lullabies. Little Oliver was no exception. When he was four years old and had just learnt to go beyond the safety of his mother's hut he had to join his brothers and sisters in the fields outside.

Herding calves was just one of little Oliver's duties. His father owned cattle which were regarded as the wealth of the family. Every night the cattle and the calves were separated. The cattle went into a large enclosure called a cattle kraal. The calves were put into a smaller kraal next to the big one.

At sunrise the bigger boys took out the cattle and drove

A herdboy from Oliver's district, in the 1920s

them away for grazing. The little boys then took the calves out to graze around the homestead. When the older boys brought the cattle home in the afternoon the milking would begin. The milking was done by one of the older boys, an uncle, or even by Oliver's father. But Oliver remembers an important duty that he had when the milking took place: "Our task was to let out each calf and during the milking we would keep the calf away from the sucking while the milking would be going on." The calves were allowed to suckle* a little, but would then be taken away from their mother before they had sucked out all the milk. Then the boys would continue milking.

After the milking the younger boys would join their older brothers and uncles looking after the cows and goats as they grazed. The grazing needed much of the boys' attention but they also found the time to sneak in a few games.

A favourite game was to stand on a hill and throw a knife at a moving target. They also enjoyed moulding toy wagons and oxen from river clay. They would then span these oxen and wagons together. The clay toys looked just like their father's wagon that trundled in and out of their village on its exciting journeys to the surrounding villages.

But sometimes the boys became so absorbed in the game that they forgot to watch the cattle. By this time the cattle would have made their way into a neighbour's field and would be happily eating up their maize or corn!

And if another neighbour happened to be passing by and caught sight of this carelessness he would quickly snap a long branch from the nearest tree, creep up to the boys and give them a hiding to remember.

Any grown-up had the right and duty to punish wrongdoers. After all you were a child of the community and every man in that community was a father to you, every woman a mother. This encouraged children to be obedient, polite and helpful not only to their parents but to the whole community.

Oliver grew up and soon took his place among the bigger boys. Now it was his turn to herd the family's cattle. Oliver Tambo remembered once or twice having to flee from an angry man: "The cattle that I was herding had strayed into a field and he chased me for quite a distance! At some point he gave up and I was saved from what would have been quite a severe beating."

Oliver enjoyed this work and he did it differently to the way it had always been done. He always searched for fields where the grass was long and lush and green. Sometimes these grazing fields were hidden in between the fields of corn and mealies. To bring the cattle from one field to the next he would have to take them through the field of mealies. No herdboy ever tried this because the cattle simply thought that they were being invited to a mealie party and ate up the lot!

Oliver began to train his herd not to eat the mealies. This training took some time but the herd did eventually learn that they were not allowed to eat the crop. Of course there was always some animal who could not resist a succulent mealie stalk. When Oliver was not looking they would try to have a quick snack. But the wily Oliver would be watching from behind a bush and a guilty sheep or goat would soon feel Oliver's stick on its nose!

From clay oxen and wagons Oliver was soon old enough to

harness* the real beasts; inspanning his father's oxen for special journeys. Oliver had to learn how to choose oxen, how to make them stand in a row and how to make them keep still while another boy put straps around them. This was no easy task. Sixteen stubborn beasts had to be put into eight orderly pairs. It took a while to master this work but with a great deal of scolding from his father, young Oliver became an expert at it.

Oliver's father left his job at the Ntlazukazi store to run his own transport business. He transported goods such as mealie bags from one district to another and from one store to another. Usually this work took him away from home for two or three weeks at a time.

To accompany his father on these trips was an unforgettable adventure for Oliver: the harnessing of the oxen; the bumpy journeys over hills and along meandering rivers that took him to new places and new faces; camping along the paths and cooking food under the stars; the excitement of coming back home after two or three weeks and seeing your mother, family and friends again. And of course there were all the stories to tell envious friends.

The oxwagon, for some reason, always arrived home late at night or early in the morning – never in the middle of the afternoon. This mystery was another thrill for the boys. The oxen were put to another important use: ploughing the fields. The Tambos had enough oxen to plough the fields of mealies and corn which they planted for their own livelihood*. And it was customary to help those neighbours who did not have oxen of their own. So, during the planting season the Tambos would plough their own fields as well as the fields of some of their neighbours.

At a very early age Oliver learnt to plough under the guidance of his father. This was not an easy task. The oxen were strong and difficult to control for a little boy. But Oliver soon learnt how to control the strong beasts. His paths of upturned soil through the fields began as crude zig-zags, but they straightened out as the boy grew in confidence and strength. Soon his proud father promoted him to chief ploughman and he ploughed the fields of grateful neighbours too!

After the seeds were sown the mealie and corn plants popped through the soil in bright green rows. But with this came the hard work: weeding. None of the boys, including young Oliver, were keen to do this work; bending for hours in the intense heat to remove the weeds from around every plant. But there was a way to make the work bearable and even pleasant.

Those families who had big fields invited their neighbours to come and spend a whole day helping to weed. And to make this back-breaking work bearable, and even fun, a sheep or goat would be slaughtered, and there would be beer and other refreshing drinks for the many dry throats.

During autumn, birds invaded the corn fields and it was the job of the boys to chase them away. Armed with a stick and clay the boys waited. As soon as the birds descended the stick was bent back, the boys took aim and released a lump of spattering clay towards the birds.

In winter the harvesting began. And when the entire family – mother, father, sisters and brothers – had gathered in the crops, the cattle would be allowed onto the fields to have their own party, seeking out the leftover mealies. But another interesting idea of sharing was practised here. A family had to allow its neighbour's cattle to feast before its own cattle could do so.

When all this was over, the boys would walk through the fields in search of mealies which may have been left behind after the harvest. It is surprising just how many they always found. These overlooked treasures were then sold to a shop owner in return for a packet of sugar or a cup and saucer which the boys would proudly present to their parents. But the story did not end there. In winter, when the families were running out of food, they would go back to the trader who would sell them mealies at very high prices.

No boy in Pondoland ever went anywhere without a stick. If you walked past a neighbour's kraal and were suddenly attacked by dogs you could defend yourself, or kill a snake that suddenly crossed your path. If a boy was seen carrying two sticks it meant that he expected a fight. Three sticks meant that there would definitely be a fight! There were many stick fights among the boys of Kantolo and Oliver became quite a fighter with his sticks. But there was one fight which Oliver remembered all his life.

Ganavu was the opponent's name. He was not a very cheerful boy. In fact Oliver remembers him as a "tough, unsmiling chap for whom life seemed to be nothing but strict business."

One day Oliver challenged Ganavu to a fight. Ganavu, in his characteristic sullen way, accepted the challenge. But things did not go as well as Oliver thought they would! "Five minutes after we had started I was beginning to realize I had made a disastrous mistake! He didn't seem to feel my blows but his were stinging!"

Oliver never again challenged the invincible* Ganavu to a fight. Neither did they ever become friends. But there were many happier days that made it bearable to have the unsmiling Ganavu as a neighbour. Two festive occasions that Oliver never forgot were Christmas and weddings.

Christmas morning found an excited Oliver waking up and hurrying to join his friends among the huts. They would go walking through the village calling "Krismis bokisi!" And always their kindly neighbours, in the spirit of Christmas, would have a smile and a small gift for them.

But everyone looked forward with great excitement to the Christmas afternoon event – horse racing. Some men came to compete with well-bred, fleet-footed horses and at the end of the day walked off proudly with beautiful blankets as prizes. It was often said that men with very fast horses managed to clothe their entire family at these races!

Weddings in Kantolo were just as memorable. The excitement of a wedding day began several weeks before when two choirs began to rehearse songs for the wedding. One of the choirs belonged to the bride and the other belonged to the groom. On the wedding day there would be a competition.

Young Oliver would watch spellbound as the two choirs

rendered their songs on the wedding day: the women swayed gracefully and rhythmically to the music while their voices filled the air. Later a cow would be slaughtered, celebrations would begin at the bride's home and a few days later at the home of the groom. A popular song at these weddings was sung in English: "Isay longy to Jellico, habla am I odis."

This strange song stayed in Oliver Tambo's head for many years, bothering him like a pebble in his shoe. What did those words mean? They certainly were not English. But then what were they? And many years later he finally understood – "I sail on a ship to Jericho. How proud am I of this."

2

Oliver's schooldays

The young Oliver Tambo thought that his life would continue with its daring stick fights, its adventurous oxcart journeys, romping in the mealie fields and the milking of cows . . .

But one day his father called him aside and told him something that would set his life on a completely new path.

"Kaizana," his father announced, "tomorrow you will be going to school."

This was a surprise, but Oliver was an obedient boy and he accepted this news without any fuss. The next day his mother dressed him in his new clothes; and off he went barefoot, to the top of the hill where Kantolo school was, about half a kilometre from home.

He saw the teacher and some children at the school which had only one classroom. The teacher called him and asked him what his name was, ready to enter this into a register.

"Kaizana," Oliver said.

"No," the teacher said, shaking his head, "you have given me your home name. I want your school name."

Oliver told him that he didn't know his school name.

"Well then," the teacher said, "you must go back and ask your parents to give you your school name. You must also have a second name which should be the name of one of your ancestors. So tomorrow you bring a name and your surname."

Oliver went home and reported this to his parents. His father thought about this and told his son that his school names would be Oliver Reginald and his surname Tambo. Oliver did not know how he came to be called Oliver Reginald but he knew where Tambo had come from; it was his great-grandfather's name. So Oliver Tambo went back to school with his new names in his head, possibly trying them out on his tongue too.

After a few months of attending the Kantolo School, an epidemic broke out which tragically killed many children there. Oliver's parents feared for their son's life and sent him to Intabaengadlingomo (the mountain that eats cattle). Here Oliver stayed with his mother's cousin Stanford and went to the Kanero School. Oliver remembers this as the unhappiest time of his life.

His teacher, Mr Godlwana, was a cruel man. All day he would walk up and down the aisles in his classroom lashing away at the children with his belt. Godlwana's favourite punishment was to fold his leather belt into a loop and to lasso the terrified children. Oliver later remembered "going to school every day with a stiff and painful neck. And every day I knew that I, like the others, would again feel Mr Godlwana's belt."

This ordeal lasted for a whole year before the epidemic in Kantolo ended and it was safe for Oliver to go back home. He was happy to say goodbye to the cruel Mr Godlwana and he had at least learnt to read and write.

Then his father sent him to the Embhobheni School. This school was eight kilometres away from home and there were a few other children from Kantolo who also went to Embhobheni. Oliver found life at Embhobheni much more pleasant than at that place where the mountain eats the cattle and the teacher beats the pupils. Oliver liked his new teacher, enjoyed his lessons and made many friends.

But Oliver remembers the nervousness they all felt on the days when the inspector came to visit the school. The pupils all waited, casting their eyes far off into the distance to look for the speck of dust winding its way along the dirt road and, as it came nearer, a droning sound could be heard. The noise stopped, a door opened and closed and the white inspector stepped out of a car. Now they all would be tested to see how much they knew!

This anxious waiting for the inspector was too much for everybody's nerves. As the inspector approached, voices could be heard. "Chamgao!" a voice at the back would plead. "Chamgao!" a girl in the front would shout. "Chamgao," Oliver would ask. The teacher would nod his consent and those who had called "chamgao" would run out of the classroom.

Was this a new language that the children were learning? Yes, it was. In English these little Xhosa children were in fact saying, "Please teacher, may I go out?" but the sentence had shrunk like a dead snake in the sun and now all that came out from a child desperate to go to the toilet was "Chamgao?" But neither the chamgaos, nor the teacher, nor the inspector could help Oliver through his tests that year.

When a disappointed Oliver went home to tell his father that he had failed, Mzimeni was angry, not at his son but at the teacher and the school.

"You must leave that school," he told Oliver. "You don't go back there again. You will now go to Ludeke." The decision had been taken. Oliver's term at Embhobheni School had ended. When the new year began he registered at the Ludeke Methodist Mission School. This was a big school which went up to standard six. There were many classrooms, teachers and even mistresses. This made life for Oliver new and exciting. But Ludeke had one big problem: it was sixteen long kilometres away from home, and to walk that distance twice a day killed a lot of the excitement that Ludeke promised. And the rainy season brought a new harvest of problems for young Oliver. He often got soaked to the bone and had no choice but to sit it out in the classroom and try to concentrate on lessons while his clothes dried on his body.

Oliver's parents realised that their son was not happy. But as always his father had a plan. He arranged for Oliver to stay with a family who lived near the school. In return for taking care of Oliver his father had to give the family a bag of maize from time to time. But no sooner had a bag of maize been sent then the family would ask for another, and another, and so on. What was the matter with this family? Maybe the sight of the young Oliver Tambo was giving everyone around him an enormous appetite.

Oliver was soon back home and once again taking the sixteen kilometre walk to and from school. He was not at all happy. Oliver's parents could see how reluctant their son was to attend school. But Mzimeni was determined that his son should learn. There was a way to encourage Oliver to attend school. The Tambo family owned several horses, and Gersey was the pride of the family. This was Mzimeni's special horse, a beautiful stallion which might have won for Mr Tambo several blankets on Christmas Day. Mr Tambo told Oliver that he could ride Gersey to school on some days.

Riding Gersey to school was a thrill. It did make school a little more appealing. But only a little. Oliver played truant and longed to be back with his friends herding cattle and playing in the mealie fields and on the hills of Kantolo, or even going to look for work somewhere beyond those hills.

Sometimes when he did play truant he would join his friends in the fields and then go home in the afternoon as if he had been at a desk all day.

"And how was school today?" his parents would ask.

"I learned well," Oliver would answer. His parents could neither read nor write so they could not check his books. They had to take his word for it. But despite his unhappiness at school and his poor attendance Oliver did manage to pass his standard three examinations in 1929. That was his last year at the Ludeke Methodist Mission School.

One day Oliver was keeping himself busy around the yard. His father was sitting near the entrance to his hut and talking to a stranger. There was nothing unusual about this; strangers often came by for food or water or to bring messages. Oliver took no special notice of the man. But this stranger was about to change his life. "Oliver," called his father. Oliver left what he was doing and walked over to see what his father wanted.

"Would you like to go to a boarding school in Flagstaff?" Mzimeni asked.

"Yes, father," Oliver replied immediately, his heart leaping with the exciting thought of going to live at a school far away from home. Mzimeni smiled. At last it seemed that his son was looking forward to being educated. And Mzimeni was right. Oliver was so excited about the idea of going to a far away school and living there that for weeks he nagged his father.

"When are we going, father?" Oliver would ask.

"Next week," Mzimeni would reply.

When "next week" arrived Oliver would be jumping all over the place with excitement but nothing would happen.

But eventually, one Saturday morning they finally set out for the long journey to Flagstaff. Oliver and his brother Alan also would be attending the school. Oliver Tambo was about 12 years old when he set off on one of the most important journeys of his life. He had left the district of Bizana never to go back there again except on school or other holidays.

Oliver, Alan and their father arrived at Holy Cross on a Saturday afternoon in 1929. The moment he had so impatiently been waiting for had at last arrived. He began to see, learn and experience new things from the very beginning.

The next day he went to church. He had never been inside such a huge building before. He marvelled at the high roof and the length of the church. After the service the congregation made a procession which ended at a nearby cemetery. This was all very strange to Oliver: some people held crosses and everyone sang. He learnt that this procession was to celebrate Easter Sunday. This was another new discovery for Oliver: he had never heard of Easter before.

Oliver soon began to enjoy his schooling very much. The principal of Holy Cross was a friendly man who encouraged the students to work hard and often found time to enjoy a game of football with the boys.

One of the first friends Oliver met at the school was a cheerful boy called Mdhlamba. Oliver and Mdhlamba were washing dishes soon after Oliver arrived when Mdhlamba challenged Oliver to a stick fight. Oliver accepted the challenge and soon the two boys were lashing away at each other. Neither boy lost but when the fight was over a friendship began which lasted many decades.

The many other boys and girls made life at Holy Cross stimulating, interesting and full of laughter and fun. Oliver's attitude to education changed and he grew to love books and the exciting worlds that they opened up for his eager and curious mind. He often scored top marks in his exams and was also a keen athlete.

Oliver spent five years at Holy Cross and became one of its top students. But the last two years at this school were frustrating. Oliver was forced to remain in standard six because he did not have any funds to move on to a higher standard at another school.

He was not the only student to be affected in this way and Holy Cross provided these frustrated students with new schoolwork to make their lives as stimulating as possible while they waited.

Oliver had applied to two schools. One of them accepted him, but he did not have money to continue with his education. To add to his woes* he ended up in hospital for a minor operation. But here his luck changed. Miss Tidmarsh, a friend and member of staff at Holy Cross, visited Oliver in hospital and told him about a school in Johannesburg where he could go and study. Oliver had just had an operation on his chest and Miss Tidmarsh pointed out to him that the high altitude provided by the highveld would be good for his health.

School in Johannesburg! A place where people went to work, to dig for gold deep into the bowels of the earth. Who had ever heard of going to school in Johannesburg! And what did the place look like anyway? He would know soon enough.

Later that year Oliver heard that he had been accepted at St Peter's Secondary School in Rosettenville, Johannesburg. A close friend of Oliver and a fellow student, Robert Sinqisha, had also been accepted at St Peter's and the two friends travelled together on the long journey to Johannesburg.

For this new, exciting chapter in Oliver's life his elder brother bought him the first pair of shoes that he had ever owned.

They rode by bus to Kokstad – the biggest town that Oliver had ever set eyes on; the streets criss-crossed endlessly and lights blinked everywhere! From Kokstad the two boys took a train to Pietermaritzburg. This was yet another new experience for Oliver: not only had he never travelled in a train before but he had never seen one in his entire life.

From Pietermaritzburg they took another train to Johannesburg. The following day they reached the City of Gold. Oliver could only stare in wonder. He had thought Kokstad to be a big city but Johannesburg made Kokstad look like a tiny village.

On arrival at the boys' hostel at St Peter's, Oliver was struck by the fluency with which all the students spoke English – as if it was their mother tongue. At Holy Cross the students had all been taught English as a school subject but had spoken Xhosa to each other. But here the students had conversations in English and spoke without struggling over any words or phrases.

In the dormitory a lively, talkative boy saw Oliver get undressed and slip under his blankets.

"Hey," the boy called to Oliver, "don't get into that bed before you put on your pyjamas!"

Oliver was surprised at the boy's words. He did not have pyjamas to sleep in. But it was not this that had surprised him. He was astounded by the speed with which the boy had uttered these words, and by the way he had used English: if the boy had spoken Xhosa he would have said, "Put on your pyjamas first before going to bed." Instead he had mentioned the bed before the pyjamas.

There was still so much to learn!

But Oliver learned quickly and worked hard. One particular incident accelerated his growing confidence among these articulate students. Ceylon Tea was promoting their product and visited the school to give the students lessons in how to make a good cup of tea. After these lessons the students were invited to write an essay on how to make a good cup of tea. Oliver's essay, to his surprise, won first prize, beating those of even the older students!

While he was studying at St Peter's Oliver's parents died. First his mother died and he had hardly recovered from this sad loss when news arrived of his father's death the following year. What made the loss all the more difficult for Oliver were the huge sacrifices that his parents had made to educate him. His father had been ridiculed for herding cattle himself while Oliver was learning at one school or another. Oliver had been looking forward to repaying his parents, to show his gratitude for the sacrifices they had made. He never got the chance to do so.

At St Peter's Oliver proved to be a brilliant student and matriculated with a first class pass in 1938. Soon he was on his way to the University of Fort Hare, in Alice in the Eastern Cape. Fort Hare was the only university in South Africa for black students. When Oliver wrote his matriculation exams he had already been accepted at this university. This was because of his excellent Junior Certificate results two years earlier. Oliver's hard work had earned him a place among the top students nationally and St Peter's was very proud of him. Oliver decided to study medicine and become a doctor. But he would find out later that the South African Government's race policies would not allow this.

Fort Hare did not offer a medical degree. It did offer a six-year course in what was called Medical Aid. On completion of this course black students could then proceed to do a degree at a white university – if a white university would accept them. In the meantime white students could go straight from matric and study for a medical degree. All this would have taken far too much time and so Oliver opted instead to do a Bachelor of Science degree.

The University of Fort Hare produced many outstanding and well known South African men and women. Among these people was a man who became a lifelong friend and comrade of Oliver Tambo – Nelson Mandela.

Mandela and Tambo were both on the Students' Representative Council at Fort Hare. This gave them the opportunity to get better acquainted with each other, through debates and other student activities.

Mandela remembers these moments quite vividly. But he also has a memory of a more frivolous* meeting with Oliver

Tambo. On Rag Day, the students marched from Fort Hare to Lovedale collecting money for charity. The students were dressed up in traditional clothes. Nelson wore the colourful clothes of the Tembu, the Xhosa tribe he belonged to. Oliver dressed in Pondo clothes and was swishing away with sticks in a pretend fight.

Oliver Tambo completed his BSc degree at Fort Hare. He then enrolled to do an education diploma. But soon after this, in 1942, students went on strike against lack of communication between themselves and university staff. Oliver, a student leader, was involved in this strike. He was expelled from university before he could complete his teacher's diploma.

The ANC Youth League

3

After his expulsion from Fort Hare, Oliver returned to St Peter's School as a science and mathematics teacher. Tambo's students remember him as a highly intelligent and gifted teacher. Tambo had an unusual style of teaching. He discussed his lessons with his students and allowed them to arrive at the conclusions themselves. This method of teaching stimulated and empowered the students, and made them exercise control over what they were learning. Tambo was to use his teaching methods to great effect when he led the ANC during its many years in exile.

Here at St Peter's Tambo met a man who would become a lifelong friend and a staunch fighter of the Government's racial laws. Father Trevor Huddleston, an Anglican priest, was a member of the school board at St Peter's.

The young Oliver Reginald Tambo

In the early 1940s, while he was teaching at St Peter's, Tambo joined the African National Congress (ANC) together with Nelson Mandela, Walter Sisulu, Anton Lembede and Robert Resha. The ANC had been formed in 1912 to resist and protest against the oppression of African people. Africans could not vote for the government and much of their land had been taken by the government for use by whites. Their lives were made difficult by laws which forced them to carry passes. Passes were permits to be outside certain rural areas known as "native reserves". Africans could not get certain skilled jobs such as mechanics, electricians and carpenters which were reserved for white workers only. These things made Oliver angry and he promised himself that he should fight against them until justice was restored in South Africa.

At about this time, one of Oliver's new friends, Sisulu, realised that Oliver Tambo was a highly intelligent man with a capacity to work hard. One day Sisulu and Tambo were talking. "Our people are always in trouble with the law," said Sisulu, "but there are so few African lawyers to help them. Someone like you – educated and politically aware – should study to become a lawyer. There is so much useful work you could do." Tambo thought about what Sisulu had said and decided to register for a correspondence course in law.

In April 1944 after a series of meetings between young ANC members and the ANC leadership, the ANC Youth League was formed. Lembede, Tambo, Mandela and Sisulu immediately criticised the ANC for the way in which it had conducted the struggle up to now.

The ANC, they argued, was weakly organised and had failed to become a mass-based organisation which should involve all African people in the struggle for freedom.

Many years later Tambo recalled the hard work that went into forming the Youth League: "There were no dances, hardly any cinema, but meetings, discussions every night, every weekend."

Anton Lembede was elected President of the Youth League. Lembede had fine leadership qualities: he was a highly intelligent man and a fiery speaker who inspired confidence and resolve in his followers. Tambo was elected Secretary of the League.

Lembede, Tambo, Mandela and Sisulu then had to convince the ANC that the Youth League should be a part of the executive of the ANC. This would enable the Youth League to participate in making important decisions for the organisation.

Dr Xuma was the President of the ANC at the time. Together with Professor ZK Matthews, and other ANC leaders, he had recently drafted the African Claims document. This document called for the abolition of the Pass Laws and demanded that African people should be given the vote. But not much was being done beyond this.

The Youth League planned to galvanise as many African people as possible in a national struggle with African Nationalism as its doctrine. It resolved to fight to remove all discriminatory laws and for full citizenship for African people so that they would have direct representation in Parliament.

Land would be divided among all farmers and peasants of all nationalities in proportion to their numbers. There would be free, compulsory education for children and a mass programme of adult education. The aims of this programme were to liberate the African people and to enable Africa "to make her own contribution to human progress and happiness".

A pamphlet calling on all youth to participate in the fight for freedom showed the new energy and determination of the Youth League. It was signed by Tambo and his colleagues in the League and read:

TRUMPET CALL TO YOUTH

The hour of youth has struck. As the forces of National Liberation gather momentum, the call to youth to close ranks in order to consolidate the National Unity Front becomes more urgent and imperative. 1944 marks an epoch in the struggle of the Black people of South Africa. A dramatic turning point in the history of mankind signalled by the global war now being waged, presents a clarion call to the youth of the Sub-Continent to rally round the banner of the National Liberation Movement so as to galvanise and vitalise the National Struggle.

In the mid-1940s the Communist Party and the Natal and Transvaal Indian Congresses were growing stronger and more militant. They wanted to co-operate with the ANC in struggling against the Pass Laws and other forms of oppression and in building trade unions. Dr Xuma was happy to co-operate with these organisations, but Oliver Tambo and other Youth Leaguers were opposed to working with non-Africans as they thought it would water down their ideology of pure "Africanism".

The year 1945 saw the Second World War come to an end. Hitler's Nazi* Germany and its allies had been defeated. South African soldiers had made an important contribution to this victory – and this included African, coloured, Indian and white soldiers, many of whom had lost their lives in the war.

The government had promised African soldiers many things in return for serving the country during the war. The Pass Laws would be scrapped and African people would be given land. These promises were never kept.

Members of the Youth League were now on the executive of the ANC and soon began to use the muscle which this status gave them. At an ANC annual conference they tried to force African Communists to resign from the Communist Party if they wanted to remain members of the ANC. Their reason was that Communists saw the struggle for liberation as being between capitalists and the workers. This form of liberation struggle, the Youth League believed, prevented Africans from seeing the need to unite in their struggle for liberation. But the Communists included such respected ANC leaders as JB Marks, Moses Kotane, Edwin Mofutsanyana and Gaur Radebe. The Youth League's motion was defeated.

This did not deter Tambo and his colleagues in the Youth League from their Nationalism. They still believed that Africans should form the vanguard* of the struggle. They accepted that some whites were against oppression, but the majority, they felt, supported it. As for Indians and coloureds, their oppression differed from that of African people and therefore their struggle should be different.

But the Youth League's attitudes would change as political events unfolded. The Youth League wanted the ANC to take radical action by demonstrations, boycotts, strikes and defiance of the law in order to free the African people. They soon found that their strongest allies in the ANC were the African Communists who co-operated closely with non-African Communists and other radicals. As time passed, Tambo and others developed a respect for the Communists as well as other non-African radicals who showed such great determination to fight oppression.

Walking out of Park Station one afternoon in 1948, Oliver Tambo and Nelson Mandela bought a newspaper. Its front page carried news that was to dramatically affect the lives of all black South African people.

Oliver Tambo and Nelson Mandela in Addis Ababa, 1961

The Nationalist Party, under the leadership of DF Malan, had won the "Europeans Only" general election. Under the United Party's Jan Smuts African people had simply been neglected and shoved to one side. But Malan had promised a programme of full-scale separate development: Whites Only cinemas, Whites Only public toilets, separate schools and job reservation. African people would now be oppressed as never before.

"Look at what they've gone and done now," Mandela said, turning to Tambo. Of course both men had known that this was coming, but here it was at last, in black and white.

"Maybe it's a good thing," Tambo said wistfully. "It might make us more determined to fight for our freedom."

By this time the Youth League President Anton Lembede had died after a long illness. AP Mda had been elected as the League's President and Tambo was elected Vice President. Mandela was elected Secretary.

In the meantime Malan showed that he meant business. Soon "Europeans Only" signs were becoming visible in public amenities everywhere: park benches, beaches, etc. By 1949 Tambo and his Youth League colleagues had drawn up a Programme of Action. They now had to convince Dr Xuma that the people were ready to fight. But the ANC leader had a more conservative style and might not like their plans. Xuma, a highly qualified medical doctor by profession, believed that the struggle should be conducted within the law as the ANC had always done. This included drawing up petitions, going to speak to the government and holding legal demonstrations.

One night, shortly before the ANC's annual conference, Tambo, Mandela and Sisulu went to see Xuma. They tried to convince him that a new chapter now needed to be opened in African politics: a chapter of action. They reminded Xuma about Gandhi. The Indian leader had involved the masses in their struggles, and not just a handful of men who knocked on the white man's door begging for their freedom.

Dr Xuma was a committed leader. But these young men were planning to break laws in their campaigns. Dr Xuma was not pleased with this new way of fighting. Under Xuma's leadership the ANC had a healthy bank account and its membership had grown. It did not need this dangerous kind of politics that would surely lead to conflict and jail.

But Tambo and his colleagues were determined to go ahead with their plans. They issued an ultimatum*; they told Dr Xuma that if he did not support their Programme of Action they would not vote for him as President-General at the coming elections. This warning did not bother Xuma too much.

At the conference held in Bloemfontein where the ANC had been formed in 1912, the Youth League carried out their plan. Dr Moroka, a member of the ANC, had expressed approval for the Youth League's Programme of Action and they voted for him as President. Of course Dr Xuma still had a lot of support in the ANC. But when the votes were finally counted Dr Moroka was the ANC's new leader. The Youth League received a bonus at this meeting: eight League members were elected to the ANC's National Executive Committee with Sisulu as General Secretary. The Youth League had triumphed. The Programme of Action could now be implemented. And the ANC was on a new path of mass action.

4

Mass action

The Programme became a turning point in the struggle for liberation in South Africa. The Youth League began to implement it immediately. The Programme included plans for boycotts, strikes, civil disobedience and non-cooperation. As the League planned all these actions Tambo must have been reminded about his student days at Fort Hare and the strike that led to his expulsion. Well, this time the issue was about the dignity of all African people in the country.

The Programme kicked off with a plan to organise a national strike; a one day protest against the Government's racial policies. The one day strike was planned for May Day 1950. There was a lot of work to be done and the Youth League sprang into action. There were people to be informed countrywide, pamphlets to be written and meetings and discussions to be organised.

Members of the Communist Party also worked hard, and separately from the ANC, to plan the strike. The Communists received a lot of publicity from their involvement and this angered the Youth League. Tambo, Mandela and Sisulu wanted the strike to promote their ideal of African Nationalism.

The Government was making plans too: it banned all demonstrations and deployed two thousand police in an attempt to disrupt the strike.

The first of May dawned. Trains were empty, factories were deserted, few people milled about on the city streets. The strike had been a success. But the day did not end without incident. Police attacked gatherings, organisers and "scabs"* brawled and riots were reported in some places. At the end of the day eighteen people, including children, had been shot dead by the police.

The Communists and members of the South African Indian Congress had helped in organising this important stayaway. Sisulu had already been convinced about the participation of these groups in the struggle. But now Tambo and Mandela also began to change their minds, seeing the need for all the opponents of the government to co-operate.

This strike did not deter Malan's National Party Government. In the same year, 1950, it tightened its apartheid policies by passing a barrage of repressive bills: the Group Areas Act, the Population Registration Act, the Suppression of Communism Act and the Unlawful Organisations Bill.

If people did not understand what these new laws meant they were soon to find out in a most humiliating way. The Group Areas Act for example, forced coloureds, Indians and Africans into separate group areas. To do this people had to be classified into race groups and many faced the humiliation of cruel Government officials pushing pencils through their hair: if the pencil remained then the person was an African, if the pencil fell out this meant that the person was coloured.

The Suppression of Communism Act made the Communist Party illegal and it became a crime to be a member. But it also had implications for the ANC. Under the Act groups or individuals could be prosecuted for trying to bring about "any political, industrial, social or economic change ... by the promotion of disturbance or disorder ..."

The ANC began to work to fight these brutal laws. This resulted in the Defiance Campaign. The movement chose six of these brutal laws and, on 26 June 1952, people countrywide were called upon to defy them.

Thousands of volunteers joined the campaign. But many feared a brutal response by the police. On the eve of the campaign churches were filled with people praying that the campaign would proceed peacefully. African Defiance volunteers deliberately walked through "white" entrances at railway stations or demanded service at "white" counters in the post offices. Indian, coloured and white supporters of the campaign entered African townships without a permit.

The police arrested hundred of campaigners. Prisons in some areas were so full that the police were forced to tell some people to go away. In Port Elizabeth a confused magistrate did not understand why people had deliberately broken the law, knowing they would be jailed. He sentenced the Port Elizabeth campaign leader, Raymond Mhlaba, to thirty days in jail while others were imprisoned for fifteen days.

The campaign achieved two important benefits for the fight against apartheid: the United Nations declared South Africa's racial policies a threat to world peace, and the ANC's popularity increased tremendously. Before the campaign its membership was around 7 000. It now grew to almost 100 000 after the campaign.

The government reacted by arresting and banning many of the campaign leaders. It passed laws which made it possible to impose fines, floggings and long terms of imprisonment on people who defied the law. The ANC decided to end the Defiance Campaign soon afterwards.

Soon after the Defiance Campaign the ANC called a meeting of the small but active groups of whites who supported the liberation struggle. Oliver Tambo addressed the 200 whites who attended the meeting. He appealed to them to form an organisation so that their opposition to apartheid would be more effective. A new organisation, the Congress of Democrats (COD), was formed and it became a close ally of the ANC.

While Oliver Tambo had been a very central organiser in all the ANC's campaigns, he had also been studying law. In the midst of the defiance campaign, Tambo and Mandela had already set up the first black law firm in Johannesburg. This is how Oliver Tambo remembers those days in the fifties:

MANDELA AND TAMBO said the brass plate on our office door. We practised as attorneys-at-law in Johannesburg in a shabby building across the street from the Magistrate's Court. Chancellor House in

```
┌─────────────────────────────────┐
│                                 │
│     MANDELA AND TAMBO           │
│       Attorneys-at-law          │
│                                 │
└─────────────────────────────────┘
```

Fox Street was one of the few buildings in which African tenants could hire offices: it was owned by Indians. This was before the axe of the Group Areas Act fell to declare the area "White" and landlords were themselves prosecuted if they did not evict the Africans. MANDELA AND TAMBO was written huge across the frosted windowpanes on the second floor, and the letters stood out like a challenge. To white South Africa it was bad enough that two men with black skins should practise as lawyers, but it was indescribably worse that the letters also spelled out our political partnership . . .

For years we worked side by side in the offices near the Courts. To reach our desks each morning, Nelson and I ran the gauntlet of patient queues of people over-flowing from the chairs in the waiting room into the corridors. South Africa has the dubious reputation of boasting one of the highest prison populations in the world. Jails are jam-packed with Africans imprisoned for serious offences – and crimes of violence are ever on the increase in apartheid society – but also for petty infringements of statutory law that no really civilised society would punish with imprisonment.

In these offices Oliver was often reminded of his own childhood in Kantolo. On a daily basis men with grey beards and weather-beaten faces would come into the offices in Fox Street. These were "peasants from the countryside who came to tell us how many generations of their families had worked a little piece of land, from which they were now being ejected."

But these many hardships that Oliver saw his people suffer both politically and in his legal work, were far from over. The majority of white South Africans were unsympathetic.

And so, in 1953, the National Party's Strijdom was elected South Africa's new Prime Minister. When asked what the Government was trying to do with the system of apartheid, Strijdom said that apartheid had been enforced to ". . . regulate life between black and white, to eliminate friction between the two groups and to ensure the safety of the white minority while at the same time providing scope for Africans in their own territories and in separate townships in the white man's area."

Chief Albert Luthuli succeeded Moroka as President of the ANC in December 1952. Chief Luthuli had already noticed the deeply committed and intelligent young Tambo in the Youth League. The two men worked very closely together and out of this friendship grew a mutual respect. It was Luthuli who in 1953 appointed Tambo to be on the commission to redraft the ANC constitution which needed to be modernised.

When JG Strijdom became Prime Minister in 1954, the two men discussed what this meant for the African people. "Mark my words, Oliver," Luthuli said, "things will become worse for us now. We have a long, tough struggle ahead." He was right. In April 1955 schoolbells rang for the last time in black private schools as the Government took direct control of education for Africans. The Government's Bantu Education law, passed in 1953, was implemented. Many people saw Bantu Education as a way of capturing the minds of black children and feeding them an education that would turn them into subservient*, uncritical adults.

The ANC was swift to announce that it would boycott Bantu Education. The Minister of Bantu Affairs, Dr Hendrik Verwoerd warned the ANC about their boycott. "Children who boycott Bantu Education will lose their places at school which will be filled by others," Verwoerd said.

"Who will these others be?" Oliver Tambo asked in an interview in the newspaper *New Age* in January 1955. "Does he perhaps imagine African parents will be eager to send their offspring to schools of apartheid where the doctrine of African inferiority will be imprinted on their impressionable minds?"

Front page of a 1960 edition of New Age

In the same interview Tambo announced that "the ANC is preparing instruction of all its branches on the implementation of the resolution condemning Bantu Education." A limited boycott of schools began soon after this interview. But the boycott had little success. Communities, parents and teachers who supported the boycott wanted to know what would happen after the boycott? Questions like this made the ANC realise the importance of planning their protests more carefully.

Among the many schools that would now be taken over by the Government was St Peter's where Tambo had learned and taught. But Father Huddleston had the school closed down rather than see it being used by the apartheid Government.

Next to be implemented was the Group Areas Act. Before the National Party had come to power in 1948 segregation had already existed. But the National Party implemented this with more rigidity. One of the first victims of the Group Areas Act was Sophiatown in Johannesburg. Tambo, whose close friend Father Huddleston took care of this parish*, knew it well. People of all races lived in Sophiatown without racial conflict.

But apartheid had decreed that Sophiatown would be a residential area for white people. On the corner of Morris and Victoria Roads in Sophiatown was Freedom Square. This is where the ANC held its protest meetings. Every Sunday the chants of *Mayibuye!* would resound for miles around as Robert Resha and other ANC speakers called on the people to resist the removal from Sophiatown and called on the Government to upgrade living conditions in the township.

Between 1955 and 1957, 58 000 people were removed from Sophiatown. A new suburb was built for whites which was named Triomf – the Government had triumphed.

"Let us speak of freedom"

5

In 1955 Professor ZK Matthews suggested a campaign to the ANC that would involve many thousands of people in the fight against apartheid. Professor Matthews had seen the white Government seek mandates* from white people in election after election. Now he saw a way to involve oppressed people in the struggles fought by the ANC and its allies.

At the ANC's annual conference in the Cape, Professor Matthews put forward the idea of a Congress of the People. He described his idea as a "National Convention representing all the people of this country irrespective of race or colour, to draw up a Freedom Charter for the democratic South Africa of the future."

Tambo was immediately convinced by Professor Matthews's idea. He realised how effective it could be in getting mass support from the ground. In 1953 Tambo had called on white people to form a democratic organisation to help fight apartheid. The Congress of Democrats was started after this call. Now here was a campaign that would involve all races on a large scale.

Chief Luthuli was also in favour of this idea. He saw it as a means of thinking creatively about the country, and of defining more clearly what the liberation movement was aiming at.

When Luthuli talked about the liberation movement he was referring to the ANC and its allies: the South African Indian Congress (SAIC), the Coloured People's Organisation, the white Congress of Democrats and the newly formed South African Congress of Trade Unions (SACTU). Together these different and racially formed organisations called themselves the

Congress Alliance and began to work together toward the National Convention.

For several weeks they went knocking on the doors of the houses of the rich and the poor. They were received into the huts in the rural areas. They held meetings in the streets, in the factories and in people's homes. They worked in Johannesburg, Durban, Cape Town, every nook and cranny of the country. The call to people was written in a poetic language:

Let us speak of the wide lands and the narrow strips on which we toil. Let us speak of the brothers without land and the children without schooling. Let us speak of taxes and of cattle and of famine.

LET US SPEAK OF FREEDOM

The people responded with enthusiasm. Their demands were written on scraps of paper, on the backs of cigarette boxes, in school exercise books. On Saturday, 25 June 1955, three thousand people gathered on a patch of open veld in Kliptown, south of Johannesburg to give birth to the Freedom Charter. Read out to the many delegates in many languages, its aims were:

The people shall govern
All national groups shall have equal rights
The people shall share in the country's wealth
The land shall be shared among those who work it
All shall be equal before the law
All shall enjoy equal human rights
There shall be work and security
The doors of learning and culture shall be opened
There shall be houses, security and comfort
There shall be peace and friendship

The Government also sent their representatives to the Congress of the People – in the form of the Special Branch, the secret police. They searched speakers and members of the audience. They confiscated banners, posters and even documents including two notices from the foodstall which read SOUP WITH MEAT and SOUP WITHOUT MEAT. But the Freedom Charter was here to stay.

The Freedom Charter boosted the morale of thousands of South Africans. It gave them something definite to work towards, and for the first time in the country's history it steered the struggle in a non-racial direction.

But not everyone in the ANC was happy with the Freedom Charter. Robert Sobukwe and Potlako Leballo were among these people. "South Africa belongs to all who live in it, black or white," the Charter proclaims. That is not true, said Sobukwe. South Africa belongs to the African people. The white people were settlers who had stolen the land from its true owners. Sobukwe, Leballo and others eventually broke away from the ANC to form the Pan Africanist Congress (PAC).

Tambo, Mandela and Sisulu had formed the Youth League with the very ideas that the PAC still held dear. But over the many years and during the many campaigns in which they worked with white people, they recognised the importance of involving all people in the struggle against apartheid. Now Oliver was not convinced by Sobukwe's and Leballo's ideas.

"The great road forward is lit up by the Freedom Charter," Oliver Tambo wrote in a report to the ANC's annual conference in December 1955. He went on to speak about the importance of this document:

"The Freedom Charter has opened up a new chapter in the struggle of our people. Hitherto we have struggled sometimes together, sometimes separately, against pass laws and Group Areas, against Bantu Education and removal schemes. With the adoption of the Charter all struggles become part of one: the struggle for the aims of the Charter."

A new chapter in Tambo's personal life had begun too. A young girl, Adelaide Tsukudu, had joined the ANC Youth League and had agreed to speak at the opening of a branch in George Gogh. Adelaide spoke about the need for black people to be represented in Parliament. Afterwards Oliver went up to her and congratulated her on her speech. A few weeks later Adelaide received a letter from Tambo, again congratulating her. She was quite surprised by this unexpected attention being paid to her, but soon Adelaide forgot about the letter. Later she received another letter from Oliver asking her why she had ignored his first letter. Adelaide could no longer ignore the determined Oliver and a courtship began.

More campaigns and the wedding

The ANC campaigns against apartheid continued. Tambo as one of the senior leaders followed them all closely, giving guidance and advice whenever necessary. Black men had carried passes. Now it was the turn of their wives, mothers and sisters.

The Federation of South African Women (FEDSAW), which included the ANC's Women's League, fought against the issuing of passes to women. They had seen the suffering and humiliation it caused among their men; men were stopped in the street by arrogant young policemen and told to "produce". Men who did not have their passes with them were sent to jail. To get one's pass in order meant standing in long, tiring queues, being ordered around by white clerks and being sent from one office to another.

This humiliation did not happen in the street only. There were also pass raids. Police burst into homes demanding to see pass books. On 9 August 1956 the President of FEDSAW, Lilian Ngoye, led a march of 20 000 women to the Union Buildings in Pretoria. There they handed over a petition to the Government.

But their warning to Strijdom that "You have struck a woman, you have struck a rock!" went unheeded by the Government. Soon African women were lining up to have their photographs taken. They had joined their men as bearers of the hated pass.

This did not stop the women from taking up yet another fight against apartheid. They demonstrated against the prohibition to brew beer. Apartheid had ensured that jobs be reserved for white people. Women had to find their own ways to supplement their families' meagre incomes. One solution was to fetch bundles of washing from white families in the suburbs, bring these home and wash them for small payment. The Government saw no harm in this: white "madams" were being given a few extra hours a week for leisure. But the women also brewed beer as another way of earning a few badly needed pennies. The Government in the meantime built beerhalls for African men. The profits from these municipal beerhalls would fill the Government's coffers and help pay for its apartheid structures. Women in Cato Manor were angry. They protested and once again the police responded with batons and bullets.

In Alexandra township people protested against a one penny increase in bus fares. For three months, under the slogan "*Azikwelwa!* – We will not ride!" people marched the twelve kilometres to work and the twelve kilometres back. After three months the campaign stopped when business subsidised the bus fares which remained at four pence.

But while the ANC continued its campaigns against apartheid, the Government was making other plans to stop them for all time. Since the Congress of the People the police had made over a thousand raids, seizing countless documents. And in the early morning on 5 December 1956, 156 Congress leaders countrywide woke up to the sound of loud banging on their doors.

Oliver Tambo, Nelson Mandela, Walter Sisulu, Lilian Ngoye, Albert Luthuli and many others all over the country were arrested and charged with treason. The Treason Trial dragged on for four long years. The trialists were granted bail, but it caused great disruption and hardship to all of them. Many could not see their families for long periods as they had to stay in Johannesburg to attend the trial almost on a daily basis.

Tambo and his law partner Mandela had great difficulty doing their legal work during this period. But Duma Nokwe and Godfrey Pitje came to the rescue and helped in the Mandela and Tambo law office. Nokwe and Pitje were friends and members of the ANC.

But the Treason Trial could not disrupt plans that Tambo had begun a few years before on the day that he first set eyes on Adelaide Tsukudu. Oliver and Adelaide were married during the Treason Trial. Even on that special day of their lives, the apartheid Government interfered. On their way to the church, the bride, groom and best man were detained for failing to produce their passes. But Tambo saw to it that they were speedily released, and so the wedding happily went ahead.

Oliver and Adelaide Tambo with friends on their wedding day

As the trial proceeded, the men and women were found not guilty and released in groups of four or five as the State's case slowly collapsed. And by 1961 all the trialists had finally been released.

In 1958, while the Treason Trial was in progress, Luthuli was voted President of the ANC for a third time. Oliver Tambo was elected Deputy President. In the same year Oliver Tambo and a friend, MB Yengwa, were arrested for not having their passes.

Driving to the police station, the two black policemen began a conversation. "Do you know about these two African lawyers who have started this law firm in Fox Street, in town?" one cop asked his friend.

Oliver pricked up his ears.

"Yes, I have," the other cop nodded.

"Well," the first cop said, "one of the partners is a guy I really like, Oliver Tambo . . ."

"Do you know this Tambo fellow?" Oliver said.

"You shut up," the first cop said to him. "You are under arrest so keep quiet."

At the police station the policemen asked Oliver for his name.

"Oliver Tambo . . ." came the calm reply.

The policeman's jaw dropped that night, and stayed that way for quite some time. But stories about the hated pass were seldom amusing. In 1960 both the ANC and the PAC began their anti-pass campaigns. The ANC called on people to burn their passes and set 31 March as the date on which this should be carried out. The PAC chose 21 March as their date. On this day thousands of people heeded the call and made their way to police stations where the protest would be carried out.

In Sharpeville, a black township east of Johannesburg, thousands of people gathered at the local police station. The mood was festive, protesters laughed and joked, a helicopter hovered overhead. Without warning the police opened fire, killing 69 people.

The political turmoil that followed caused widespread panic in white communities. A few days later the Government declared a state of emergency and over 2 000 people were detained. On April 8 both the ANC and the PAC were banned.

This banning did not come as a surprise to the ANC. They had already begun to plan ahead. And Oliver Tambo was probably the most important part of these plans. When the Sharpeville massacre happened, Tambo was doing ANC work in Cape Town. He received an urgent message from Chief Luthuli. There was reason to believe that the ANC may soon be banned. Tambo was instructed to leave South Africa immediately to win international support for the ANC's cause.

Into exile

The ANC had decided that it would need an ambassador to promote their cause to the outside world. The organisation had chosen Tambo to undertake this important mission. Oliver had proven over the years that he was one of the ANC's best leaders for this task. He was articulate, committed and had a vast knowledge of South African as well as world politics. His sharp mind and a keen sense of strategy* were balanced by his quiet and thoughtful manner, his sense of humour and his ability to listen carefully to the arguments of his opponents. Tambo was a man who was able to work with people of different backgrounds and ideologies. He would be suited to working in the international scene.

"But you have to leave immediately," Chief Luthuli stressed. "And secretly, as many people all over the country are being picked up and jailed." Tambo immediately began to plan his escape. Ronald Segal was a close friend of Tambo, editor of the provocative opposition journal *Africa South*, and a member of the Congress of Democrats. Segal's parents were wealthy business people who went about their business in expensive cars driven by a uniformed chauffeur.

Tambo quickly contacted Segal and told him about the urgent message from Luthuli. The two men sprang into action. Segal stole his parents' car and a chauffeur's uniform. If any security policemen saw the smart car cruising northwards up to Johannesburg on its way to Bechuanaland, all they saw was a black man in a peaked cap and a white man lounging beside him. What they were looking at was in fact the escape of Tambo and Segal.

Tambo's and Segal's next stop was Wattville in Benoni where they informed an anxious Adelaide about their plans. Adelaide packed some clothes into a suitcase and bid her husband a safe journey. She would join him later that year with their babies, Thembi and Dali.

The 1950s had seen the Congress movement change from protest politics to defiant mass action: from petitions to the burning of passes. Tambo's steady rise in the ANC to its highest leadership positions proved how effectively he was able to respond to the crisis in South Africa. It also indicated the confidence that the Congress had in his abilities. But the 1960s would test his skills as never before.

Oliver Tambo, possibly in the late 50s, on one of his many overseas missions to promote the liberation struggle in South Africa

One of the first African leaders whom Tambo saw was Kwame Nkrumah of Ghana. Nkrumah was a respected and admired leader who had led his country to independence and had become its President in 1960. Ghana was the first African country to achieve independence from colonial rule.

The ANC needed the support of countries such as Ghana and Nkrumah advised Tambo to form an alliance with the PAC. The ANC and PAC had many unresolved differences. But Tambo believed that the priority now was to get rid of apartheid. He took Nkrumah's advice and the United Front was formed.

Tambo worked hard to make the United Front an effective organisation. He travelled all over Africa and spoke at the United Nations, calling on countries to support the struggle against apartheid.

But the United Front did not enjoy a long life. The differences between the PAC and ANC made it hard to work together outside the country. "We were an odd body," commented Tambo after its break-up. "We were united outside, but were representing organisations which were not." Nevertheless, he felt that the Front had served its historic purpose for a time, and that was to put the fight against apartheid on the international agenda. Oliver Tambo wrote a letter outlining these problems and managed to smuggle it to the ANC inside South Africa. Mandela and his comrades there agreed that the Front should be dissolved. After eighteen months it folded.

Tambo attended the Commonwealth Conference in London in 1960 with one specific goal, to convince the Commonwealth* that South Africa's racial policies were incompatible with those of Commonwealth members. South Africa should therefore be expelled. South Africa did not wait to be expelled. In 1961 South African whites held a referendum to decide whether or not to become a Republic. Urging white South Africans to say "Yes" to a Republic, Prime Minister Verwoerd assured them that: "This is our country, our government, our commercial and industrial life, our mines, our agriculture, everything is ours together."

On 10 December 1961 Chief Albert Luthuli was awarded the Nobel Prize for Peace. At almost the same time the ANC and other members of the Congress were planning the beginnings of a different kind of struggle: sabotage.

After blowing up a few electricity pylons with home-made

bombs, the ANC decided that this method of struggle was far too ineffective. Nelson Mandela slipped out of the country to go and plan the armed struggle and to form Umkhonto we Sizwe, the military wing of the ANC.

When he came back into the country he went to report on his activities to Luthuli. But on his way there he was arrested. He was sentenced to five years in prison for inciting workers to strike and for leaving the country illegally.

Before he could complete his sentence, Mandela was brought to trial, together with Sisulu, Ahmed Kathrada, Govan Mbeki and several other Congress members. On the very day the Rivonia Trial began – 8 October 1963 – Tambo addressed a Special Political Committee of the United Nations General Assembly. In his address he said: "Today some thirty persons are appearing before a Supreme Court judge in South Africa in a trial which will be conducted in circumstances that have no parallel in South African history, and which, if the Government has its way, will seal the doom of that country and entrench the feelings of bitterness which years of sustained persecution have already engendered among the African people . . ."

Tambo went on to urge the United Nations not to stand by calmly watching what is "genocide masquerading under the guise of a civilised dispensation of justice." But it would take many more years before people all over the world would stand up and do something to end apartheid rule. Mandela, Sisulu and others were sentenced to life imprisonment.

Oliver Tambo was in London, many of his comrades were in prison on Robben Island and he was thousands of kilometres away from the masses of the people, who had for years themselves been the main weapon in the struggle against apartheid.

The ANC had to find a new base from which to operate. Oliver Tambo went to Tanzania and was allowed to set up a base there. Scores of young people had left South Africa in answer to an ANC call to join Umkhonto we Sizwe (MK) and undergo military training.

After a few months of training these MK soldiers were ready to return home. But this was not so easy: there was no internal leadership to come back to. Nor could they wage an armed struggle from South Africa's borders as these were ruled entirely by colonial governments who were friendly with the South African Government.

But in one of these neighbouring countries, Rhodesia, an armed struggle for freedom was being fought: the ANC decided to fight alongside the Zimbabwe African People's Union (ZAPU), led by Joshua Nkomo. The plan was to fight their way southwards and enter South Africa. Two major campaigns, the Wankie and the Sepolilo Campaigns were launched.

While these campaigns were being planned Chief Luthuli died unexpectedly in South Africa. Chief Luthuli and Oliver had been very close friends and had seen many struggles and campaigns in the ANC. Luthuli had led the ANC with dignity and a deep commitment which had won the organisation many followers and friends. In honour of President Luthuli Oliver Tambo named the first detachment to cross over into Rhodesia the Luthuli Detachment.

Those soldiers had undergone military training in the Soviet Union and in Zimbabwe. Now they were going to fulfil their dreams to fight their oppressors at home. But this dream did not materialise. Many were killed while others were captured and sentenced to life imprisonment in Rhodesia. Some managed to escape to neighbouring Botswana. But the Botswana Government arrested them and they too were jailed. Among these men was Chris Hani.

When Hani and other ANC soldiers were released from prison they returned to Zambia. But they were not happy with what they saw there. Many of the ANC's leaders had settled in townships in Zambia and Tanzania, where they were preoccupied with solidarity work and international work. In the meantime trained ANC soldiers were languishing in the camps in Zambia. It seemed to many that the struggle inside South Africa had been forgotten.

Chris Hani presented a strongly worded petition to the

leadership. This led to a conference in Morogoro, Tanzania in April 1969.

This conference lasted a week. Over seventy delegates from the ANC and its allied organisations attended. The leadership was severely criticised for allowing the struggle to slow down. Many members of the ANC executive were enraged by these criticisms. But Tambo believed that many of the criticisms were valid and wanted a fresh evaluation of the ANC's progress in exile. He and the entire executive resigned their positions and new elections were held. Tambo who was highly respected by ordinary members was immediately re-elected President. They valued his leadership and believed that the organisation needed his skills.

Among the important resolutions passed at the conference was the formation of a Revolutionary Council to oversee the day-to-day direction of Umkhonto We Sizwe. Another resolution passed at the conference was that non-Africans – coloureds, whites and Indians – could join the ANC as individuals although they could not be part of the ANC

Oliver Tambo with Samora Machel of Frelimo in Maputo

executive. This resolution would lead to more tension within the leadership of the movement.

Soon after the Morogoro Conference certain members of the ANC executive led by Tennyson Makiwane accused Tambo of being a poor leader. Comparing Tambo to Samora Machel of Frelimo they said: "The world sees Machel in battle fatigues while our leader is always dressed in a suit and carrying a passport." But the more serious reason for the dissension was that the ANC had decided to allow non-Africans to join the organisation. Robert Resha, an old friend of Oliver's from the Youth League days was also against non-African membership. While these arguments continued Resha died. The dissidents chose Resha's funeral in London to publicly attack Tambo for allowing non-Africans to join, especially members of the SACP.

This was an all too familiar argument to Tambo. He must surely have recalled his own strong opposition to non-Africans and the SACP in his youthful days in the forties. But he had travelled a long road with many faithful and committed people from other racial groups and the SACP, including key strategists such as Moses Kotane and JB Marks, who were fully committed to the ANC. Oliver believed, as the Freedom Charter stated, that South Africa belonged to all who lived in it.

Unity, he thought, is the most important thing to keep in mind. We must always strive to keep our movement united and to unite as many of our people as possible around our main goal: the destruction of apartheid and the establishment of democracy in South Africa. This theme of unity always remained central to Tambo's thinking.

But this was not always easy. Over the next six years Makiwane and a group of seven others who opposed the ANC's non-racialism, disrupted activities. It was decided to expel them from the organisation. Tambo was saddened by this, but had become convinced that it was better to be rid of the group than to allow the activities of a few people to divert the whole organisation from its main tasks.

The group of dissidents led by Makiwane was expelled from the ANC in October 1975.

Meanwhile, after years of fighting the ANC, the political balance was shifting significantly against the South African Government. This process began with a series of wildcat strikes* in Natal, the Transvaal and the Cape in 1972 and 1973. In neighbouring states, Frelimo in Mozambique and the MPLA in Angola began their guerilla war against their oppressive governments. This inspired black people inside South Africa who saw other oppressed people fighting oppression and racism.

And another philosophy had begun to take root inside the country under the leadership of Steve Biko. Black Consciousness was a philosophy of black pride and a commitment to the fight for freedom. The ANC's efforts to gain international support began to make an impact: at last governments in Asia, Africa, Europe, and the Scandinavian countries began to speak out against apartheid. ANC offices and representatives were established in several countries. The ANC, with Tambo as its head, encouraged the many anti-apartheid groups that sprang up amongst ordinary people in Britain, Holland, the USA and many other countries. The ANC had called for international sanctions against South Africa. Now its higher profile was giving the important campaign more and more momentum. In 1974 the United Nations General Assembly refused to allow South Africa to take its seat. This marked the beginning of the changing political tide: of an arms embargo against South Africa and cultural and sports isolation.

At the end of 1975 the South African Government's Department of Bantu Education instructed all secondary schools to use Afrikaans as a medium of instruction for half their subjects. Before this all subjects were taught in English. Despite student resistance to this the government went ahead with its plans.

On 16 June 1976, Soweto students went on a peaceful march in protest. Police fired on a group of these marchers and suddenly the country was engulfed in the worst turmoil it had ever known. At the end of 1977, when the police guns stopped blazing, over 600 people had been killed.

Back in Lusaka, Oliver Tambo called the ANC leadership together to discuss the crisis in South Africa. "We must be ready to lead our people at this time," he said. "We have to ensure that young men and women who leave South Africa in search of military training are provided with it in MK. Those who want to continue their studies must be given the opportunity. The ANC must open its doors to receive all those who leave South Africa, and we must establish a strong underground organisation* to carry on the struggle inside the country."

In two different ways, contact between the angry youth of 1976 and the ANC was made during and immediately after the Soweto uprising. Scores of Black Consciousness leaders and supporters were arrested and imprisoned on Robben Island. There they met Mandela, Mbeki, Sisulu and the other ANC leaders who had been in prison since the early sixties. Many of these youths were converted to the ANC's cause.

Another group of youths crossed the South African border to join Umkhonto we Sizwe and took up arms against the South African police and army. These young people left their parents and brothers and sisters at home in South Africa. They soon realised that life in the ANC training camps was not easy. Food was scarce, and even though many came from poor homes inside South Africa, they found even fewer comforts in the camps.

But here OR (Oliver Reginald), as Tambo came to be affectionately called, showed another skill that made him a popular leader. He often visited the training camps and took a personal interest in each youth there. Whenever the camp inhabitants heard that OR would be visiting them there was

OR with MK Chief of Staff, Chris Hani

great excitement. And when he finally arrived he spoke to every soldier personally, remembering little details about each person from his last visit. Although fiercely militant, these young people often missed their families desperately. OR was their loving father figure who understood their dreams. "He had the gift," remarked his close personal assistant, Neo Moikangoa, "of making everyone feel special."

Tambo himself badly missed his own family, whom he saw once or twice a year when he passed through London. Adelaide Tambo, now a highly qualified matron, was supporting the family, which included a third child, Tselane. Adelaide was working double shifts – night and day – in a famous London hospital. The children were sent to boarding school. Adelaide was a strong woman, and independent; yet she clearly adored her husband. Whenever ANC comrades came to London, she would offer them hospitality and beg for news about Oliver. Tambo also deeply appreciated his wife's contribution – since the ANC took up all his time, he was not able to be the family breadwinner.

His wife's grit* reinforced Tambo's respect for women, who so often had to shoulder many burdens. In the ANC itself, Tambo made a point of practising affirmative action for women, grooming them for high positions, sending them for training and education to institutions around the world. "Oliver Tambo," observed Lindiwe Mabuza, ANC Chief Representative to Sweden and the USA, "had the ability to draw out people's latent talent." Tambo himself pointed out that "it is the responsibility of both men and women to work for the emancipation of women."

The late seventies and early eighties saw people inside the country begin to organise: trade unions, civic groups, women's groups and youth groups began to form, demanding better pay, houses, schools and amenities. And in 1980 the ANC made its presence felt. Umkhonto we Sizwe set up a top secret Special Operations committee. This committee reported directly to Tambo. The best MK soldiers were chosen to hit strategic targets inside South Africa. Bombs exploded at police stations, major oil installations and even at Voortrekkerhoogte, a large South African army base near Pretoria.

The Nationalist Prime Minister, PW Botha warned of a "total onslaught" against South Africa and retaliated by conducting hot pursuit raids into Angola. Innocent civilians in Botswana, Swaziland, Mozambique and Lesotho were killed in the SADF's bombing attacks. The South African Government's plan was to destabilise its independent neighbouring countries. It wanted to make them economically and politically dependent on South Africa and stop them supporting the ANC. It funded, for example, the anti-Frelimo guerillas in Mozambique – Renamo – helping them to raid rural people and attack the railways that linked Zimbabwe to its neighbours.

There were also death squad operations. Throughout the 1980s, ANC members were assassinated. These included academic Ruth First, killed by a parcel bomb in Maputo and Dulcie September, ANC representative shot dead in the streets of Paris. There were many others. On 9 December 1982, the

SADF raided Maseru, Lesotho, killing 42 people. Tambo was outraged by the massacre, but despite pleas for him not to go near a country which was surrounded by South Africa, he attended the mass funeral on 19 December to show his support for the grieving families.

"What OR's presence did for us who remained, for those who lost loved ones and those visitors from home who came to bury their friends and family . . . for our wonderful Basotho hosts," wrote Phyllis Naidoo, who was an exile in Maseru at that time, "no pen can adequately describe."

Ten days later, MK guerillas attacked the Koeberg power station, near Cape Town. In the following year, MK guerillas blew up an airforce base and a police building in Pretoria – an act which received spectacular publicity. A week later, the SADF bombarded a suburb in Maputo, killing 58 people.

Destabilisation also affected the ANC. It came to light that scores of spies had infiltrated MK and had provided the enemy with the information which had led to the massacres. They were put into special camps for observation. But the attacks continued and created a damaging atmosphere of tension.

There was growing pressure from other countries for the South African Government to reconsider its racial policies. But the Botha Government steadfastly refused to speak to the ANC or any other popular political groups in South Africa. Instead it hatched a plan which would appease its white voters and ease international pressure. This plan was to install a "tricameral parliament" which would give coloureds and Indians token power in government.

This solution had the opposite effect: it intensified campaigns against the Government and led to the formation of the United Democratic Front in Cape Town. Trade unions, civics, women's youth and student groups came together in one united front to fight apartheid as one cohesive force.

The ANC was of course still a banned organisation. But anyone who cared to listen to the voice of its President Oliver Tambo could do so by tuning in to Radio Freedom as it broadcasted its bold messages on a weak and often disrupted frequency from Lusaka in Zambia: "In this coming period we shall have to pursue with even greater vigour the destruction of the organs of government that will render the country ungovernable."

In 1985 township youth took up this call with enthusiasm. In Port Elizabeth and the surrounding areas they called for a mass stayaway against an increase in the price of petrol.

The stayaway was almost one hundred percent successful. But it did have a tragic end. On 21 March, the 25th anniversary of the 1960 Sharpeville massacre, police opened fire on mourners at a funeral, killing 21 people.

Angry crowds reacted by burning the homes and cars of black community councillors and policemen in the townships – people seen as the State's functionaries and collaborators in state brutality.

The violence spread across the country in unending spirals of demonstrations, police brutality, funerals. The Government tried to control this "unrest" by declaring a state of emergency.

Hundreds of young people decided, as they had done in 1976, to leave the country and join Umkhonto we Sizwe. But MK, as the armed wing of the ANC was called, had already intensified its infiltration into the country. MK soldiers bombed police stations, government buildings and even restaurants. Many innocent civilians were injured or killed in these attacks.

Oliver Tambo was unhappy that MK was now going for soft targets inside the country. He called MK leaders to a meeting and demanded an explanation. Chris Hani and Steve Tshwete explained that it was sometimes difficult to communicate with MK members inside South Africa. But an angry Tambo did not accept this excuse. It was he who had to explain these actions to the world, saying that this was not official ANC policy, but the anger and frustration of youth on the ground.

In the ANC detention camps, too, tension was mounting as assassinations occurred and hit squads continued to kill. Embittered camp minders began to abuse their inmates, even though their guilt as enemy informers was not always proved.

Eventually, news of these abuses reached Tambo. Deeply disturbed he ordered an urgent investigation and the worst excesses were stopped.

But Tambo was not able to monitor the camps more closely. His workload was increasing dramatically, damaging his health. He suffered a mild stroke from the pressure of travelling, interviews and supervising the ANC offices worldwide. Realising that the spiral of violence was beginning to affect the moral integrity of even the oppressed, he was constantly on the move, urging the world to increase sanctions against South Africa if it wished to see an end to the violence in the country.

As tensions mounted the country's economy was plunged into a deep crisis: unemployment, poverty and rising prices. People everywhere began to despair. South Africa was no longer a haven for those white people who had always depended on the Government and the police to keep the country safe and happy. White businesspeople realised that they would have to look beyond the Botha Government for solutions. The cracks in the once invincible pillars of apartheid were beginning to appear.

As the leash of power began to slip out of the hands of the Government, the people began to grip it firmly in their own. In 1986 the Congress of South African Trade Unions was formed. At the launch of the largest trade union federation in the country, its president called on PW Botha to release Nelson Mandela. Soon after its launch COSATU went to speak to the ANC in exile about working towards a democratic South Africa.

As the Government structures of black local authorities broke down, these too were replaced by the people who formed their own street committees.

But these transformations were not always smooth and painless. In 1986 the world watched in horror when activists executed alleged sell-outs and informers with the "necklace" method. A motorcar tyre was doused in petrol, placed around the victim's neck and set alight. Countries all over the world began to realise that only the ANC would be able to influence the mass of the people inside South Africa. Tambo himself condemned the necklacing, calling it "barbaric", but the Botha Government refused to allow newspapers to publish his statement.

But now, Tambo was being invited by heads of major powers for consultations. He held interviews with President Mikhail Gorbachov in Moscow and the Commonwealth representatives in Britain, as well as the Secretary of State of the USA in Washington.

In October 1986, the US Congress overruled President Reagan and voted to impose official sanctions against South Africa. Oliver Tambo's long and patient work with the anti-apartheid movements had begun to take effect. Ordinary people, through their campaigns in European and American countries, made it clear to members of the Botha Government that they were not welcome visitors. South Africa had become the polecat* of the world.

From inside South Africa, a steady pilgrimage of trade unionists, religious leaders, businesspeople, academics, artists, writers and sportspeople openly made their way to consult with Oliver Tambo and the ANC. PW Botha's Government was thoroughly isolated, both from the world as well as from within.

Over the years, Tambo had been conducting secret communications with Nelson Mandela and the other political prisoners on Robben Island. Now, together, they agreed that the time had come to begin negotiations with the South African Government. Tambo had to convince the Government that the only way to bring peace and stability was to sit down and talk. But a difficult task faced the leader of the ANC. For many decades thousands of people in the ANC and its allied organisations believed that an armed struggle would bring the apartheid Government down. Now Tambo had to convince people inside South Africa, Umkhonto we Sizwe in the camps, and the many African and Western governments that negotiations had to begin.

9

Towards freedom – the last mile

Tambo decided that a document had to be drafted by the ANC which would include the conditions for negotiation with the South African Government. Several long months of consultation followed. Steve Tshwete, a senior member of the ANC recalled the last days of this work. Kenneth Kaunda had lent Tambo his private plane and Tshwete and his colleagues Penuel Maduna, Thabo Mbeki and Pallo Jordan accompanied Tambo on his visits to Tanzania, Zimbabwe, Botswana, Angola and Mozambique. After weeks of flying around to these countries, long hours of meetings, debates, arguments and more meetings the Harare Declaration eventually began to take shape. Back to Lusaka they flew to work until the small hours of the morning. This document was taken to the Organisation of African Unity (OAU), debated further and finally issued by the OAU on 21 August 1989.

A few days before this, Oliver Tambo suffered another stroke from the enormous pressure of work – this time a lot more serious than the first one.

Tambo needed sophisticated medical treatment which was unavailable in Zambia. Kenneth Kaunda offered a jet to fly OR to London, where his wife, Adelaide, was anxiously waiting to care for him. But when Tambo's Swedish friends heard about what had happened, they insisted he be flown to Sweden to be treated in their best hospital.

Adelaide reluctantly agreed to be parted from him, feeling that this was in her husband's best interests. He was then flown to Stockholm.

The intense political activity that followed had to take place

Oliver Tambo is re-united with comrades and friends after the unbanning of the ANC in 1990

without him, but he had laid the basis for a negotiated revolution.

A few months later, the South African President, FW de Klerk, announced the unbanning of the ANC and other organisations. Nelson Mandela was released from prison, as were other political prisoners. Exiles began to return to South Africa.

Chief among the returning exiles was Oliver Tambo. The ANC Youth League organised a jubilant reception for him when he arrived at the airport in Johannesburg. The ANC Youth League immediately declared him their Honorary Life President. At the ANC's National Conference he spoke to delegates about the long years in exile, the changes that the movement had undergone, and what it had achieved. He ended his address with these words: "We were always ready to accept our mistakes and to correct them. Above all we succeeded to foster and defend the unity of the ANC and the unity of our people in general. Even in bleak moments we were never in doubt regarding the winning of freedom. We have never been in doubt that the people's cause shall triumph."

And so, after more than thirty years outside the country, OR Tambo had returned. His entire family returned with him. Adelaide Tambo had a joyous reunion with her brothers and sisters, and with their old friends in Wattville, Benoni. The children, speaking with English accents, faced the task of getting to know their parents' beloved country. Thembi was now a young mother of four. Dali and Tselane, professional artists in television and the theatre respectively, had inherited their father's creativity. But OR had also brought back with him the ANC and said to the people, "Here it is, intact, and with hardly any scratches and blemishes. It is yours, take it, but take care of it as I did."

Under his special guidance, the ANC, despite its many diverse followers – Africanists, Communists, liberals – had stayed together. Tambo had succeeded in making each member, whether young or old, man or woman, artist or soldier, feel that they owned the liberation movement. And all the time, through his collective leadership, he challenged them to fight with fierce determination, for freedom *would* come. Yet, he commanded, liberation must come with as little cost to human life as possible. Through the Harare Declaration, he had delicately steered the ANC from revolutionary resistance, through to the difficult path of revolutionary negotiation.

Thousands throughout the world had come to love and admire Oliver Tambo. Heads of state were his personal friends. He inspired ordinary people of many countries to play their part. For them the ANC symbolised the fight against racism, which existed to a greater or lesser extent throughout the world. In South Africa, despite the banning of his image, his name and his words, he had become a household name.

Oliver Tambo returned to South Africa in poor health. In the 1980s his health had begun to deteriorate. But at the ANC's Kabwe Conference in 1985 he vowed: "Whatever little is left of my health will be consumed in struggle." The final hammer blow came with the death of Chris Hani which affected him deeply. At the ANC's July conference in 1991, Nelson Mandela was elected President while OR took on the less demanding job of National Chairman.

Just two weeks later OR was admitted to the Milpark Hospital in Johannesburg with a chest infection. Soon afterwards he suffered a severe stroke and died.

He was buried at the Wattville cemetery, near the town where he lived many years ago, after a moving ceremony attended by thousands of people, at the FNB Stadium near Soweto.

Thousands of South Africans and dignitaries representing virtually all governments of the world attended the funeral. Oliver Tambo was like Moses, preached the Reverend Frank Chikane. He had seen the promised land from the mountain, but died before he could enter it. His life-long friend and comrade, Nelson Mandela, paid a loving tribute. Oliver Tambo, he said, was the "jewel in the crown" of the ANC. He went further: "I say that Oliver Tambo has not died, because the

Old friends meet again. Nelson Mandela and Oliver Tambo

ideals of freedom, human dignity and a colour-blind respect for every individual cannot perish." Then he made a solemn promise to his fallen comrade:

> "As you commanded, we will defend the option of a peaceful resolution of our problems.
> As you instructed, we will bring peace to our tormented land.
> As you directed, we will bring freedom to the oppressed and liberation to the oppressor . . .
> In all this, we will not fail you."

Learn new words

Commonwealth – an association of independent states that used to be governed by Britain (page 42)

frivolous – not serious (page 16)

grit – courage (page 50)

harness – the straps and fittings by which an animal is controlled and fastened to the cart that it pulls (page 5)

homestead – a house and other building, usually traditional, on communal land (page 2)

invincible – something or someone that cannot be defeated (page 7)

livelihood – a way in which a person earns a living (page 5)

lobola – a gift paid to the family of the bride by the groom (page 2)

mandate – authority given to a person or group to perform a certain task or apply certain policies (page 32)

Nazism – the reactionary policies of the National Socialist (Nazi) party in Germany which was brought to power by Adolf Hitler in 1933 and which led to World War Two (page 21)

parish – an area or community which has its own church and priest (page 31)

polecat – to be unwanted and remain an outcast. A polecat is literally an animal which smells terribly! (page 54)

scab – a worker who chooses not to be part of a strike action – sometimes referred to as a "sellout" (page 25)

strategy – a plan for future action to achieve an objective (page 40)

subservient – subordinate or inferior (page 29)

suckle – when a young animal feeds at the udders of its mother (page 3)

ultimatum – a final demand or request which will lead to certain consequences if it is not met (page 24)

underground organisation – an organisation that operates secretly – usually because it is illegal (page 48)

vanguard – the leaders of a struggle or movement (page 21)

wildcat strike – strikes which are unofficial and not recognised by the law and which happen without prior planning (page 47)

woes – troubles or sorrow (page 14)

Activities

Choose the correct answer

(a) Oliver Tambo was forced to remain in standard six at Holy Cross because
  (i) he failed his examinations.
  (ii) he did not have anything else to do.
  (iii) like most black children he did not have the money to go a higher standard at another school.

(b) After matriculating Oliver Tambo went to the University of Fort Hare because
  (i) it was close to where he lived.
  (ii) he could study for a medical degree.
  (iii) it was the only university for black students in South Africa at that time.

(c) Who became Oliver Tambo's closest and life-long friend at Fort Hare?
  (i) Walter Sisulu
  (ii) Father Trevor Huddleston
  (iii) Nelson Mandela

(d) What was the ANC Youth League's main criticism of the ANC?
  (i) The ANC was doing very little with all the funds it raised.

(ii)   It had failed to become a mass-based organisation.

(iii) There was no place for young people in the ANC.

(e)   Why was the ANC's conference in Bloemfontein in 1912 a turning point for the Youth League?

(i)   Dr Xuma was re-elected as president of the ANC.

(ii)   The Youth League staged a mass walkout of the conference.

(iii) Dr Moroka, who supported the Youth League's Programme of Action was elected President of the ANC.

Make your own drama

Discuss in groups why you think the ANC's Programme of Action was important. Then recreate in drama the meeting between the ANC Youth League and Dr Xuma. Refer to pages 23 and 24.

Write your own demands

Which laws did the Defiance Campaign of 1952 want to break? Name the laws and then write down sound reasons why you would have opposed these laws.

Write your own story

What major event took place on 25 June 1955, at Kliptown in Johannesburg? Pretend that you are a reporter for the *New Age* and write a detailed observation of the occasion, commenting on the mood of the people and the importance of the event. Create a suitable headline or title for your story.

5

Write, sing or rap your own praise poem

Praise poetry and songs are part of Africa's great oral tradition in which the history of a people is passed down by word of mouth and a combination of song, music and dance. Praise poetry is literally used to sing the praises of people who have made important contributions. Remember the praise poet *(imbongi)* at the inauguration of President Nelson Mandela in May 1994? Two South African poets influenced by the oral tradition are Mzwakhe Mbuli and Lesego Rampolokeng.

Now write a praise poem commemorating Oliver Tambo's contribution to the struggle for liberation in South Africa.

More books about the life and times of Oliver Tambo

Benson, Mary. 1990. *Nelson Mandela.* London: Penguin Books.

Lodge, Tom. 1985. *Black Politics in South Africa since 1945.* Johannesburg: Ravan Press.

Pampallis, John. 1991. *Foundations of the New South Africa.* Cape Town: Maskew Miller Longman.

Reddy, E.S. 1987. *Oliver Tambo and the Struggle Against Apartheid.* New Delhi: Sterling Publishers.

Tambo, Adelaide. 1987. *Oliver Tambo Speaks.* London: Heinemann Educational Books.

Illustrated History of South Africa: The Real Story. 1988. Cape Town: Reader's Digest Association of South Africa.

Ulibambe Lingashoni – Hold Up the Sun. 1993. (A set of five video cassettes produced for the ANC.) Toron and Thebe Investment Corporation: Johannesburg.